To Bu.,
Many years in
service together —
Enjoy — and use.

Jim Rhodes
May 29/86.

James R. Rhodes' POEMS

James R. Rhodes' POEMS

The Edwin Mellen Press
New York and Toronto

Library of Congress Cataloging in Publication Data

Rhodes, James R., 1922—
    James R. Rhodes' Poems.

    I. Title.
PS3568.A62A6   1982   811'.54   82-20374
ISBN 0-88946-999-7

Copyright © 1982, James R. Rhodes

For information about this and other titles write:

    The Edwin Mellen Press
    P.O. Box 450
    Lewiston, New York 14092

Printed in the United States of America.

Introduction

James R. Rhodes is a poet who happens to be a Christian minister. That is why he and I happened to meet, became friends, and why I, a theologian, have the privilege of penning some introductory words to this selection of his poetry.

As a poet, Rhodes understands his calling to be first and foremost an observer. What appears as a poem from him is a translation of sights and sounds, of experiences and emotions, observed sometimes with a mind's eye, and sometimes with what he calls "the eyes of the heart" in his poem "Blind Sight." In any case, the stuff of perception from the five senses and from the full range of human emotions, from love and reverence to fear, anger and perplexity becomes the subject of reflection by his poetic sixth, or should I say 'seventh,' sense. Then it is brought to expression in lyric, rhythmic lines that need to be heard to be appreciated fully.

In his nature poems the outer world is rendered reseeable through marvelous imagery borrowed by his consciousness from other senses, such as the trumpet sound to describe a sunrise in "Day Aborning" or the multi-gyrations of a swarm of bees described as "Belly Dancing." But then things are dramatically reversed and the inner world is described in terms of the outer world in a way that refines and reconveys deep-running emotions, as in "Cry-Bones" and in "Sea Maiden" where the experience of crying is expressed as "ballet feet across my tears' terrain" and personal anguish as "welling heart-chords" furnishing music for "the dancing drumming hallways of my throbbing brain."

There are many dimensions to this man and his poetry. A keen ability to reason comes to playful expression in "Human Logic," and is genuinely celebrated in his masterful "Each Other" found at the end of this volume. A veritable feast is offered for those who in the non-lyric bleakness of contemporary one-dimensional poetry are suffering from metaphysical hunger, as in "Be or Be Not," "Self-Same Differences," "Reality" and "You Are." There are love poems here that have the power to rekindle the feelings and to drive lovers to share the words with each other and by them to reaffirm their love, as in "Catch You Catch Me Not," "The Final Falling" and "Each." The mentoring mind of a man who has lived through his mid-life crisis invites his readers to celebrate life, as in "On Maturity," "Building," "To the Prisoner," "A Person" and his marvelous "And You?"

Jim Rhodes is a man who likes to get up in the morning and to live each day as the only one, as he himself said in his meditative preface to this volume. Here he tells us the secret behind all of the need to observe, to see, to feel, to touch, to smell, to love and be loved. In these poems we walk with the observer-poet from the rising of a day, "Day Aborning," through the forest paths of his beautiful bass-ponded farm near Ballston Spa, New York, where most of these poems were written, to the seashore, "Aloning," and through a fall, winter, spring and summer season with reflections on time along the way.

We accompany him on his pastoral rounds as he visits a hospital, "Waiting" and "Patient Observation," and as he attends a dying person, "We Both Know." We are with him at a funeral, "The Last Laugh" and "Commital Day," and in the evening after burying a friend, "Charon." We join him at the communion rail, "These Faces I See," and he shares with us his theological inside, "Naming His Call," "Mystery," "Ever Beyond" and "Reformation."

Like his love poems, Rhodes' poems of faith strike fire in hearts that have the fuel for them. I have found that reading one of them from a pulpit never fails to lift hearts in joy and praise. His own heart lifted to God in his words has been a lever for many.

Here is a poet, here is a man, here is a minister for the reading! Take and read, then share with others what you find!

> Dr. Michael D. Ryan
> Drew University
> New Years Eve, 1981-82

Author's Preface

How to find time for the privacy of self alone with self? Time is a poor creature of man's own making. Who are we mortals to place draw-strings on the past and carry it with us as a distortion of the present and the evil of the future? Somehow we should be able to say each morning, "There will be but one day and this is it!"

The future does not exist. It cannot exist until it becomes the present, and at the very moment we feel the present is at hand, it has already become the past.

Yes, we can plan, and do. We can remember the past, and as memory it is never actually lost. The present is the now-ness of our lives. This sense of the now moves us to act in terms of our environment and our accumulated experiences. So, act we do—but, life has a point of cognition—a time when we become dimly, and often acutely, aware that we have lived so much in terms of the past and the future, that in reality we have not lived at all. We have never really been the self we planned for out of the past we knew because we never fully realized that in all of life there is only one day—today, and only one time—now.

The author, The Reverend James R. Rhodes, was born in 1922 in Altmar, New York. He graduated from Green Mountain Junior College in Poultney, Vermont in 1942, from Syracuse University in 1944, and from Boston University School of Theology in 1947.

He is a United Methodist minister and presently pastor of the McKownville United Methodist Church in Albany, New York. His first book, *Spring Field, and Mountain Stream,* was a volume of poems published in 1968. Other poems have appeared from time to time in Church publications and in local newspapers.

Married to the former Elizabeth Cornthwaite of Ballston Spa, New York, he is the father of four married children, and the grandfather of six.

Contents

Part One
The World Without   1

Part Two
On Time and People   17

Part Three
The World Within   39

Part Four
The Poet as Minister and Theologian   73

Part One

The World Without

Day Aborning

Blue-blares
    The Sun's
Golden trumpet
    In molten tones,
And fan-fares
    Crimson-yellow
The sleeping clouds,
    Climbing
The blue horizon
    Into day-rise—
Shattering the night
    With a shout of light
Upon a thousand hills,
    Tinting all the
Little leaves
    That tremble
Newly yellow
    In the touching breath
Of morning.
    Fresh-washed,
The dew-grass chimes
    Rainbow sounds
To celebrate
    a day aborning.

Bittersweet Brown

Bittersweet brown,
    And drifting down
The hours
    Of yesterday;
Autumn burns
    A brighter fire.

Bittersweet green
    In summer seen
To trace its leaves
    In spiral wind
On sinewed trunk
    And branched tree.

Bittersweet yellow,
    In days of brown;
Fires of autumn,
    And laughter remembered
Drifting down,
    Drifting down.

Pine-spice frangrance
    Over the ground;
Seasons of
    Bittersweet,
Bittersweet brown,
    And laughter remembered
Drifting down,
    Drifting down.

Cold, so cold;
    Bright berries
On lace-branched blue,
    Spiced needles brown;
Life's laughter remembered
    Drifting down;
Bittersweet,
    Bittersweet brown.

Whispering Harps

Flat milky-green
    Unbreaking
Still waters;
    Rain, coursing steady
From leaden skies;
    Pinnacled spruce and pine
Standing shrouded
    Along the shore line;
Harbor
    Full of silent ships
Moored
    And waiting—
Masts, fingering black;
    Water dripping
"Plock,"
    Into small pools;
Rain, coursing steady,
    Sounding the
Sibilant music
    Of a thousand thousand
Whispering
    Droplet-harps
Across a silent sea.

Aloning

Sea-gulls—
    Terns—
Blue cauldron sky—
    Gentle surf
Cross-rippling
    The sloping
Hard wet sand—
    Lovers walking
Hand in hand
    Along the
Lapping-line—
    Picking solitaire
Stones and shells
    Selected from
Oceans' bounty—
    Sand castles,
Braided kelp,
    Fishermen
Standing cold
    And waist deep
Way down
    The beach—
The smell
    Of salt,
Seaweed,
    And ocean
Wind—
    A cleanness
Upon the earth
    And in
The heart—
    A distant
Sail
    Wings the sea
With a
    Wind-blown grace
That sings
    Its sailing—
Soft mists

    Move shoreward
In the heat
    Of morning
Sun—
Lovers
    And sand-castles,
Sails and
    Fishermen,
Slowly dissolve—
    A fantasy scene—
Nothing left
    But the cries
Of gulls
    And terns,
And the
    Cleansing murmur
Of the morning sea—
These two—
    Aloning
Together.

The Last Five Flowers

The last five
    Are exceeding rare
Airy October blooms;
    Delicate beyond
Imagining—
    Invisible, unseen;
Five fall pastels—
    So shaded,
So blended,
    That they are
Beyond the
    Perception
Of human
    Sensibilities
And have never
    Been seen
By mortal eyes;
    They are
Distillate of Autumn;
    Of sun and leaves,
Clouds and skies,
    And swirling
October winds;
    They bloom
But once
    Upon a love
In a life time;
    Here!
They are yours.

Moon Maiden

Pale mystery
    Of creation's cycles,
Holder of hearts' hands
    And haunts of
Paining souls;
    Mover of deep tides
Oceans wide;
    Balm and torment
Of soft summer nights;
    Sweet caress
On misting meadows,
    Shining waters,
And green-shadowed
    Mountains
Against the golden
    Moon-blue sky.
The moon
    Is a woman—
Of a woman's mind,
    A woman's
Heart and soul;
    The hungry, loving,
Mother-maiden,
Tenderly stilling
The tumult of day
    In the quiet radiance
And possessive passion
    Of her
Moon maiden way.

Sough and Sift

The white songs
    Of wind-slanted,
Racing, whispering snow,
    Are lullaby sighs
Cradling
    Sleeping greens
Muffled beneath
    The layered down
Of silent ice
    And wind-sculptured
Curl-lipped
    Shadow drift;
Sweeping, whispering,
    Lullaby keen,
Softly-covering sigh,
    A crystal kiss—
Blown in the
    Snow songs'
Sough and sift.

Silver Sliver

High above December clouds
    A silver sliver moon
Slides through the winter sky;
    Earth below wears winter shrouds
Of crystalled grass and frosted trees
    Of star-flaked new made ice;
A sense of hurry blows the wind,
    A feel of coming snow,
While high above the gathering clouds,
    A silver sliver moon
Slides through the winter sky.

For the Wind

The wind blew
    Dark-land
Bitter
    Brittle cold,
Fierce and old
    As the storms
Of winter
    Are old;
Bare earth
    Was iron
And the dust
    Was ice
In a brown
    Whirling dervish
Along the
    Empty streets;
Blue-cold
    Crimson
Sunset bands,
    Grey-pink clouds,
And a
    Winter water
Pale sky,
    Made for the wind
An ear
    And an eye.

Thistle Down

In the arms
    Of a thistle
In the
    Thistle-down,
In the soft
    Of a
Whistle
    In-wing,
Over, and
    Under-around,
In the
    Feathers of
Faith
    And pinions
Of air,
    In the
Day-sun
    Sound,
In the
    Blue
And the
    Fair;
I nestled,
    I found—
In the arms
    Of a thistle
In the soft
    Of a whistle,
The Warmth
    And the
Peace
    Of the
Thistle-down.

Greening Song

All the world's
    A greening, a greening;
And all the world's
    A greening in spring.

Everything's new
    A meaning, a meaning;
And everything's new
    With a meaning in spring.

All the senses
    Are keening, a keening;
And all the senses
    A keening in spring.

Misty and green
    Redeeming, redeeming;
Rain misty and green,
    Redeeming I sing.

And all the world's
    A greening with meaning;
Soft misting and green,
    Redeeming I sing.

Soft O' the singing
    Sweet singing and ringing;
Soft O' the singing
    Of greening in spring.

Benediction

Soft rain
    Has a healing touch;
Soft rain
    We need so much.

Makes things
    Green and grow
That once we thought
    Were dead.

Striking gently
    The up-turned face,
A blessing
    Of heaven's tears.

No bitterness to taste,
    Only tear-washed
And wet-faced
    In warm spring rain.

Soft rain
    Has a healing touch;
Soft rain
    We need so much.

Belly Dancing

A tumescent
    Turbulence
Of swarming
    Inside;
Bumbling
    Of bees
And scheduled
    Flight
Of a
    Thousand-thousand
Bright
    Sun-warming,
Dancing and
    Swarming bees;
Crawling
    Wing-shine
Coming
    Bee-line
To the warm
    Golden light;
Belly-dancing
    Bees
Felt buzzing
    Down-blue
To sun-warm
    And honey-bound
Flight.

Part Two

On Time and People

What Time Is It?

Listen to
    Man and time,
Clocks and bells,
    And day and nights;
Shackled and manacled,
    Prisoner of dimensions
Unseen, but known.

Bound to the pendulum beat.
    Swinging the hours,
Marking the day,
    Tocking the seconds,
Turning time's tune
    Timeless.

Listen, and see;
    The very first man
Gazing in silent awe
    At the rising
And setting of the sun;
    The bright birthing
Of each new dawn,
    High-noon and life
And dark embers of
    The dying sun.

In the misty quiet
    Of liquid moon-washed
Nights—
    He must have said,
"I shall not fear
    For it will come again,
As always, before and again,
    Through the long night
Will steal the golden dawn;
    Maker of day and
        High-noon,
            And evening,

And I bow me down
    To this life of day
That brings courage
    To the death of night."

So he bowed him down
    And marked the time,
Each day to day—,
    High-noon,
And a time to worship,
    Perhaps a time to pray;
Marking the time;
    Giving the pendulum its
First push.

Swing and divide,
    Divide and divide
The pendulum beat,
    Swinging the hours,
Marking the days,
    Bowing to life,
And in fear,
    Dividing it from death;
The running prisoner
    Of dimensions unseen,
But known.

The King Is in His Counting House

The wonderful
    Greedy, lusting
Covetousness
    Of counting
Over and over
    Your wealth
Of days
    Spent and kept;
I've been counting
    All day long;
King,
    In my own
Counting room
    Behind locked doors
One may enter;
    Counting treasures
Carefully stored,
    Fondling each
Golden coin
    Worn smooth
In the tumbling
    Of times recalled;
Currencies of
    Every denomination
Between
    High-song day
And sadness;
    Coins of the realm,
"Remembered,"
    Of the times, "Two!"
Saved and hoarded
    To be counted
And recounted
    Like beloved
Prayer beads
    Touched briefly,
One at a time,
    Upon the
Bright strings
    Of yesterday.

Ceramic

Blue glaze
    Turns
Upon the wheel
    Of the Potter's
Earth and clays;
    While the Potter's
Wiping hands
    Finger tentative
Dawns and
    Sunsets
Across the
    Turning days.

Morning Song

Speak gently to the day,
    For it may well reply,
And the echo of these hours
    May darken another's sky.

Speak gently to the day,
    The sun is not yet high,
And out of dark hours past
    Hear yesterday, and cry.

Speak gently to the day,
    And gentle your reply;
Who seeks his soul in beauty,
    From you beauty buy.

And all around is harsh,
    All around is hurt and cry;
Speak gently to the day,
    And gentle your reply.

So Little Time

Life has
    So little time
To say much
    Of nothing
And everything;
    So little time,
So much
    Of nothing
And everything.
    That is,
Nothing to say;
    When all is said,
What can you say,
    With so little time
And all of life
    To say it in?

Love's Yin-Yang of Days

Monday;

Monday's fair face
    Is cradled
In the hollow
    Of Saturday's
Laughing arms,
    Her shining eyes
Changing blue-grey
    And browning skies;
Laughing free
    With her little songs
And loving eyes
    That sing to
Saturday—
    With a silent tear
Beneath her glow
    By the crows-feet
Kind,
    Jeweling joy
And laughter
    With its sweet hurt
And sadness
    Blind—
Oh, the joy of Monday!

Tuesday;

I heard the subtle
    Seaside wind
Whisper in my ear,
    Felt it softly
With my cheek;
    The voice of my beloved
So near
    I turned to speak—
To let the vagrant wind
    Repeat
And stroke
    And cool caress

    Where love's hands
        Had wandered,
Love's cheeks had pressed;
        Yet there,
Beneath it all,
        The silent tear
That gathers
        In the inward
(Corner-kind)
        Jeweling joy
And laughter
        With its' sweet hurt
And sadness
        Blind—
Oh, the joy of Tuesday!

Wednesday;

Wednesday wrote a letter
        In sands upon the shore.
And tracked upon its' pages
        The words, "Forevermore;"
Bright turning tide
        Carried Wednesday's letter
Oceans wide,
        And all the seas
Sang joy in the sun—
        Love ran the foaming tide
And watched the sunset run
        To banner evening skies,
And brighten sunset eyes,
        And then remind
That there
        Beneath it all,
The silent tear
        That wells to fall,
Jeweling joy
        And laughter
With its' sweet hurt
        And sadness

Blind—
    Oh, the joy of Wednesday!

Thursday;

Thursday, love wrapped
    Universe around,
Love locked the door
    And threw away the key;
Entered every portal,
    Flooded every hour
With its' tender fierceness
    And its' awesome power;
Love that, as love should,
    Gave, and gave, and gave,
While, captive, we received
    And shared the death of each
That each might live;
    That each might laugh
And give and reach
    With love on Thursday—
While there,
    Beneath it all,
The silent tear
    Traced love's cheeks
Jeweling joy
    And laughter
With its' sweet hurt
    And sadness
Blind—
    Oh, the joy of Thursday!

Friday;

Friday, love's
    Sweet perfume—
Love's musk remains,
    And lingering
Delights the soul
    With hours remembered

Where love was spent;
    In this treasured realm
The coins of love are frittered,
    Freely spent,
Held hand in hand—
    Sent filling
Inward selves
    With golden riches
Of times and places—
    Love's faces remembered,
Love walking intertwined;
    Yet there,
Beneath this touch,
    We find the silent tear
Jeweling joy
    And laughter
With its' sweet hurt
    And sadness
Blind—
    Oh, the joy of Friday!

Saturday;

Saturday has
    Great bandy-legs,
A pot belly,
    A green giant's laughter;
A cowrie shell
    For ocean speech,
And a yellow bird
    On Saturday's beach—
With little songs
    And echoes
That follow after
    The love of Saturday
And the giant's laughter;
    In his giant arms
Are golden leaves
    And scarlet suns
And sisters soft—

    Are smiles and tenderness,
Deep river runs
    And tumbling falls
Always to this, to this;
    Beneath it all
Love's silent tear
    Gathered by the
Crows-feet kind,
    Jeweling joy
And laughter
    With its' sweet hurt
And sadness
    Blind—
Oh, the joy of Saturday.

Sunday;

Sunday, I heard
    The blue-bells ring
While canyoned brooks
    Played organ notes
Through moss
    And branched pine;
Love wrapped itself
    In clouds and trees,
And milky-way,
    And turned
To love's sweet slumber;
    Breathing soft,
And holding warm
    All the starry smarmy
Love could capture,
    Looking to
The orbing moon,
    Touched with
Lunar rapture—
    Sunday turned and slept;
Soft, beneath it all,
    Love's silent tear
In sifting rain refined,

      Jeweling joy
And laughter
      With its' sweet hurt
And sadness
    Blind—
Oh, the joy of Sunday!

Building

Once upon a boyhood
    I sought to build
A bird house,
    It was to be
A grand and gothic
    Affair;
I could see it
    All together
In my mind,
    Gabled, roofed, and
Columned structure;
    But, somewhere,
Things went wrong;
    Boards split,
Nails bent,
    And pieces
Would not fit.

My father said,
    "You'll have to begin
All over again."
    I did, and
Boards split,
    Nails bent,
And pieces
    Would not fit.

My father said,
    "Begin again."
I did,—
    In triumph
I built—
    A feeding station
Which hung
    Nearly forty years.
In bush and tree
    Feeding birds
I would have
    Housed.

The People, Us

We,
    The people,
Who by
    Non-vote
And vote,
    Render
Ourselves
    Irresponsible:
Victims
    Of our own
Un-made
    Mandate,
The big lie,
    And fair
Sweet hope
    That vested power
Is honest
    And that
Which is
    Representative
Is both
    Moral
And wise—
    We all
Consent
    In this
Un-contested
    Consentual;
Which
    Leaves us
Relatively
    Undisturbed
Until—
    Our neighbor
Dies.

A Toast

Here's a toast
    To the games
We play
    And lives
We cripple
    Along
Cowards' way
    While pretending
Everything's
    Simply o.k.
Cool drinks
    Anyone?
Something on ice?
    For God's sake,
Whatever you do,
    Please,
Be nice!

"1984"

The Indians
    Worshipped the
Rain and water,
    Sun and forest creatures;
They believed in,
    And loved
The Great Spirit;
    But, we told them
They were wrong.

We were the pioneers,
    And in this virgin land
We sang the city's song,
    And took a "Christian" stand;

We told them
    They were wrong,—
Who worshipped
    Rain and water;
Sun and forest creatures,
    And loved
The Great Spirit;—

    Now, all of these
Are gone.

Real

It is the simple
    Beautiful
And loving things
    That are real;
Dancing feet,
    Laughing hearts,
Loving souls,
    Lifting hands,
And caring people,
    Are real;—
Real things
    Are not always seen;
Clutches at the heart,
    Breath-catchers of the soul,
Candles of the eyes,
    Cadences
Of all the ways
    That persons
Can care for
    One another;
Real things
    Are person things,
Not thing things.

Woman on a Park Bench

Dawn sifted sunlight
    And saw her
Sitting open, quiet,
    And eager;
Worn blue jacket,
    Matching slacks,
Jaunty red
    Babushka;
She fingered
    The breeze
With her smile
    To herself;
She looked
    An ocean,
Distant;
    Drank
Copiously
    Of trees,
Drifted high
    On morning
Bird-song
    And
Did it all
    With
Consummate
    Ease.

Something in the Hunter

There's a fierce
    Intelligence
In a wild thing's
    Eyes;
Bright knowing's
    Incandescence
When a wild thing
    Dies;
Hunters
    Look away
When a
    Wild thing cries,
And something
    In the hunter
Also dies.

Star-Eyed Boy

I have a star-eyed boy
    Fey-man of fifteen or so;
Almost six feet of
    Man-boy that sings
And swings with
    A sinuous grace in
Walk and dance;
    A soul of music
And a tender heart;
    A heart of fun
And a black depression
    At what the world has done.

I have a dream-eyed boy
    And a blue-eyed boy,
Fey-man of fifteen or so;
    Wide set and wide open
And questing and questing,
    And why?
A song for the singing
    And strings to play
And mankind's worries
    To plague his day.

I have a wide-eyed boy
    And a sad-eyed boy;
Man-boy of fifteen or so;
    Magic touched his man-boy face,
Open with a man-boy smile—
    A shyness to his grace,
And a soul-touched life all new.

A soul-touched life
    And a song to sing;
Blue-eyed and dream-eyed;
    Sad-eyed or wide with joy;
But most of all I have
    A wonderful star-eyed boy.

Irish Violin

Man,
    Who could not
Sing his tears
    Or cry
His pain,
    Made
A violin.

Man,
    Wrung
Exquisite
    To the mood
By one
    Violin
Sobbing
    The solemn
Beauty of
    Music,
The soul's refrain,
    Winged joy
And sadness pain.

Waiting

Emergency
    Waiting-room
People are
    So poignant
With their
    Waiting-room
Expressions of
    Deep human care;
The taut worry lines
    They wear
For someone;
    Their tired slump,
The slept-in hair
    And hunched butts
Of blackened
    Cigarettes;
The vacant stare
    Of enforced patience;
Of watching
    And waiting
Because
    They care.

Patient Observation

Dear Doctor
    Or Nurse,
As your patient
    Grows worse,
Remember please,
    That man's identity
Is more important
    Than his disease.

Part Three

The World Within

Mind Songs

Gypsy readings
    Are mind-songs
That have no sound
    But see what is
And will be;
    Silent songs
Of fortunes,
    Foretelling the
Luck and lives
    Of all the
Yesterdays
    Yet to come.

Oh, magic songs,
    Tell my fortune,
Sing your mystic
    Airs that see
And do not sound;
    Knowing, revealing,
Sensing and feeling;
    Mind-songs
That have no sound,
    But say
What we know
    In our hearts.

Look Through My Window

Fractured sunlight,
    Butterfly blues;
Wings over star-light,
    Morning-glory news.

Bells on the back door,
    Button at the front;
Home is the window
    In the picture-window hunt.

Framed for the vision,
    Window to the world;
Two-way glass
    With the shutters uncurled.

Sun-stained glory
    Dancing shadowed green;
Dark-centered pools
    Where the deep self is seen.

Rain-washed clear,
    Wind-blown blue;
Starlight centered
    For seeing things new.

Fractured sunlight,
    Butterfly blues;
Wings over starlight,
    Morning glory news.

Look through my window;
    Are you looking in, or out?
That's what our selves
    Is really all about.

On Maturity

Maturity is
    The ability
To use freedom
    Responsibly
And intelligently.

Maturity
    Is the
Acceptance
    Of life
As it is,
    And people
As they are.

Maturity
    Is a
Nice word
    For ripeness
And what
    Follows.

Maturity
    Is the
Ability to
    Accept
Criticism
    As well as
Praise.

Whose views
    Coincide
With mind,
    Is obviously
Mature.

Maturity
    Is the
Long plateau,
    The time
Of bearing
    After growing.

Maturity
    Is the
Giving of seed,
    And the
Returning of fruit
    To the
Onwardness
    Of life.

Reality

Reality is
    Warm woods soil,
Black and sweet
    Cupped in
Two hands that believe.

Reality is
    Lightning as well as
Sunshine,
    Thunder as well as
The sacred solitude of the
    Silent forest.

Reality is
    The balance
Between pain and ecstasy,
    Between suffering and pleasure,
By which each knows
    The other to be.

The ideal is
>   What ought to be
Out of the patterns
>   Of the past;
The real is
>   What is.

If you cannot believe,
>   Do not make believe;
If you cannot accept,
>   Do not pretend.

In the deepest sense,
>   Reality is love,
Because true love
>   Does not pretend
Nor does it make believe;
>   True love
Accepts what is.

Reality must be
>   Community;
It must be
>   The community
Of the senses
>   In agreement;
It must be
>   A community
Of persons
>   Seeing
The same things
>   Differently
And alike.

Soul Music

The strings of the soul
    Play a luted song,
And muted mute
    Their vibrancy
Climaxes a visceral
    Pain of the luted lute
And strung
    Between soul and brain
The startled heart-beat
    Throbs these chords
Again and yet again.

Spring-breath of violets,
    The two-touch warmth
Of holden hands;
    Sunset-snows crimson
And clouded bands—
    The heart beats beauty;
And the unsung songs
    Surge and beat within
The strings of the soul
    Playing a luted song,
And muted mute
    Their vibrancy.

Pain of the luted lute;
    And strung
Between soul and brain
    The startled heart
Knows love, sees beauty,
    Catches the breath,
And blows the strings
    Of the soul;
Playing a luted song,
    Throbbing these chords
Again and yet again.

Dichotomy

Out of the depths,
    I'm a being torn,
Life rending the spirit
    Not the flesh;
Tearing with teeth
    Of conflict
The agony of desire
    Fulfilled and lost again.

Of paradise—
    Not lost, but out of reach;
Of tormented souls
    Whose trunk-lines
Run in the same cable
    Without communication.

In the frustration of
    Love's empathy and desire
Between the generations;
    In the dark depression
Of the soul's straining
    At the threshhold of light,
And the vast ignorance
    Of the how, and why,
And whofor?

Blind Sight

The heart has eyes
    To see, to see;
Blind-sight of feeling
    In me, in me.
        And
Caught in the hinge
    Of its throbbing fist
Are all of life's dreams,
    And hope's long tryst.

For
The heart has eyes
　　To see, to see;
With a vision deeper
　　Than me, than me.
　　　And
Caught in the pain,
　　In the twist of the beat,
Are the shadows that walk
　　And the lives that meet.
　　　For
The heart has eyes
　　To see, to see,
The sadness of knowing
　　To be, to be.
　　　And
Swift to the thrill
　　Of life's deep surprise,
The heart leaps wild
　　As the heart-song flies.
　　　For
The heart has eyes
　　To see, to see
That its deepest loves
　　Are free, are free.
　　　So
Dance to its beat
　　And leap to its light;
Live to its song
　　And trust to its sight.
　　　For
The heart has eyes
　　To see, to see,
That the blindest of all
　　Is me, is me.

A Person

Instinctively,
    I know
What a
    Person is.

A person
    Is empathy
Of selves;
    The sum-total
Of another
    From their
Point of view;
    A song
Trying
    To sound
Itself;
    A cry
To those
    Who hear;
A cringing
    In fright,
Cowering
    In fear;
A need
    To be held—
To be dear;
    A person
Is love
    Seeking a
Home;
    Is the pain
Of being
    In company
With beings;
    Is eyes—

Yes!
    A person
Is eyes—

    Seeing and
Avoiding
    Being seen;
Is a
    Veiled light
Behind
    Two windows.

Courage

Courage is fear
    Taking a stand.
Courage is knowledge
    Braving the chance.

Courage is the day
    One step at a time,
And patience the strength
    For the courage stance.

Courage is calmness
    Begotten of faith,
And walks in the dark
    With no backward glance.

Courage is fighting
    The "I can!" and "I will!"
Thus, winning or losing,
    By courage advance.

Catch You Catch Me Not

Love is a will-o-the-wisp,
    And a dancing flame
Across the marsh sands—
    Consuming naught that I can see,
But fierce its burning nightly.

Watch it from solid ground;
    Stand on the safely known
And see how foolish to pursue
    A will-o-the-wisp
Through marsh and morning dew.

Who ever clutches a flame,
    Or catches a dancing fire
That comes and goes,
    And weaves a ghostly trail
Where hearts may catch travail?

Why seek, and hunt, and chase,
    And who can catch a wisp?—
Or running down the nights and days
    To weary life itself,
And cry the song of a dancing flame
    With empty soul and heart the same.

For love is a will-o-the-wisp,
    And a dancing flame,
Chasing the chaser and calling his name;
    Running him down his nights and days;
    Catching his soul and heart the same.

So cry the song of the dancing flame,
    Run chasing down your days;
For love is surely a will-o-the-wisp,
    And weaves its ghostly trail
Flame catching two hearts chasing the same.

To One Afraid

Darkness can be a friend;
    Be not afraid of the dark,
For darkness is kind to welling tears
    And hides the worried heart
In its uncritical arms;
    It brings the only privacy
Some people ever have,
    And softly comforts
Broken-hearted and
    Contrite souls.
Darkness hides the little hunted things
    In woodland haunts and trails.
Give me darkness
    In which to see myself
And no fear
    Of others seeing;
Be not afraid of the dark
    For darkness is kind.

The Final Falling

To fall in love
    Is beautiful,
Beautiful;
    You two,
Who walk
    Love's aura,
Remember,
    Walking is
A process of
    First
Standing up,
    And then,
Falling—
    Catching yourself
With your
    Best foot
Forward.
    Love is
A process of
    First
Standing up
    Together,
And then,
    Falling—
Catching
    Each other,
Best foot
    Forward.
Love is
    The final falling
In learning
    How to walk,
And run,
    And mount up
With wings
    In your journey
Together.

For Me?

I am
    A song
Not yet
    Sung,
A journey
    Incomplete,
A reason
    That
Eludes,
    A search
That fills
    Its pockets
With partial
    Things
And waits
    The twist
Of the
    Startled
Heart
    Every time
The phone
    Rings.

Cry-Bones

What I can do
    I cannot,
Yet,
    I can;
Its the will
    Against
Will not;
    The ability,
The wish
    Against
What is;
    The cry-bones
Encased
    In the flesh
Where they
    Weep unseen;
The wind
    Howling uphill
Against
    Gigantic
Ocean waves
    Only to
Smash them
    To bits
Upon the shore,
    Returning
Endlessly
    For more
And more
    Until,
Finally,
    The wind
Dies
    (calm begot)
Having done
    What it could,
And
    Could not.

At the Same Time

Love
    Is the
Wild and free
    Gift
Of being
    Willing
To become
    Absolutely
Vulnerable;
    Supreme gift,
Each to each
    Given
And received
    In a
Singing joy
    That,
To me,
    Carries a
Deep sensing
    Of tears
And awe
    And sorrow,
All at the
    Same time.

Sea Maiden

In the swirl
    And pulsing whirl,
A cadence—
    Shuddering beat
Of ballet feet
    Across my
Tears' terrain
    And down
The dancing
    Drumming hallways
Of my throbbing brain;
    A curtsy,
Fingers interlaced,
    Bowing sweetly low—
Hands placed deep
    Within red
Welling heart-chords
    To pluck sweet pain
Of music lost
    And found again
In the swirl
    And pulsing whirl—
Constant cadence
    Shuddering beat
Of crashing seas,
    Ballet feet,
Vaulted echos
    Ever, and ever again
Singing a
    Sea maiden's name,
Toe dancing
    Ballet feet
Across my
    Tears terrain.

Tracing

Tracing lightly,
    I would trace
The lines
    Of love
Upon your face;
    I will not
Fail to see
    The etch
Of years,
    Or tragedy,
And I shall
    Catch your
Sorrows' tears
    And sense
The suns
    Of laughter years;
But just
    This once,
I would trace
    The lines
Of love
    Upon your face.

The Image

Behold,
    My self
I see,
    But,
How do
    I see
This self
    Of me?

A flame,
    A fire,
Born as

    I became—
To hearing
    And seeing,
Doing
    And being;

Bright silver
    And gold
My lambent
    Flame and
They gave it
    A name,
My name;
    And I am
Forever bound
    To confess,
Confessing
    All my life—
That I shall
    Never, never,
Be worth less
    Than silver
And gold,
    And the
Lambent flame
    Of my
Birthing mould,
    And the gifts—
Of spirit,
    Of flame,
And a name,
    My name.

And You?

There's a child in me
    That delights
In butterfly wings,
    Stained glass windows,
Blue-green bottles
    And sun-through things.

Running half a century
    To fly a kite
And face the fingers
    Of the wind,
Hearing trees turn
    Leaf-full harps and singers.

Heart to a standstill
    Of breathless awe
At pageantry dawns and sunsets,
    Birdsong summer days and
The touching grace of
    Small animal innocence.

There's a child in me—
    Laughing and lonesome,
Loving and hurt,
    Boy-skipping shout
Through life
    In his executive shirt.

A child—
    Singing wordless chants,
Collecting wild beauty,
    Speaking nascent truth,
Living half a century
    Clothed in un-child duty.

Anything

The beginning
    Of anything
Is its
    Ending.
That which
    Is begun
Must either
    Cease, or,
Arrive at
    The reason
For its
    Beginning.

Self-Same Differences

Self facing,
    We see
In the other
    Of ourselves
The same journey,
    Same stars,
Same sunlight
    For laughter,
Same hungering hope—
    Without hurt
To quench our thirst,
    Drinking our fill
From the moiling wells
    Of the other
In ourselves;
    Knowing,
In ourselves,
    The wounding,
The healing,
    The wholeness.

You Are

Truth is
    What is;
You are,
    Therefore, truth,
For better or worse;
    Know then truth;
That truth is
    Neither good or bad,
Right or wrong;
    It simply is
The truth;
    It simply is
What is;
    You are.

Narcissus

Feeling a sadness
    That wants
To be alone,
    Intensity
Of aloneness
    That shuns
Company
    And feeds
On its own
    Black mood
Paining the
    Inward world
With the ache
    Of unshed tears;
Seeking somewhere
    The comfort
Of crying unashamedly—
    And never
Finding it.

Success

Success is
    Tired faced,
Grey-haired,
    Well suited,
Lean looking men—
    Eating lunch
Together
    At the counter;
Each on a
    Beeper-leash.

Note Worthy

Dance of
    The differences;
Contrapuntal
    To a major
Harmony
    In another
Key
    Where each
Is the
    Music
Between
    And both
Are the
    Song.

Each

Is
    Of both
To be one,
    Yet,
Each
    Be self;
Both
    To be
Bound,
    Yet,
Each
    Be free
In
    The other;
Each
    To desire,
Yet,
    Possess
Only
    In the act
Of giving.

Drop-Out

One must move
    Into the unknown
In terms of the known,
    Else,
The present has no purpose
    And the future no meaning;
    This,
In the truest sense,
    Is what it means
To be lost.

The Truth

Always lies
    Somewhere between
What is said
    And what is not said.

The Lie

Speaks truth
    Somewhere between
What is known
    And what is told.

To Be

Is both of these,
    And what is
Lies somewhere
    In between.

To Become

Is movement
    Between these
And what is
    Becomes what is—
True.

Wisdom

Is the product
    Of vision
Seasoned with
    Experience.

Up-Tight

Ulcers are the
    Unshed tears
Of yesteryears,
    And the
Unsaid fears
    Of tomorrow.

Responsible

People
    Who are willing
To make decisions
    Usually
Get blamed for them.

Clown

Obese
    Buffoon,
Lacerated
    Flagellant,
And no one sees—
    Not even in secret.

"———"

When you
    Give Him a name
He belongs to you:
    You cannot
Belong to Him.

You're Dead!

Tin soldiers,
    Toy guns,
Primitive appeal—
    War is
"Boys taught to play"
    Gone real.

See, God?

Often,
    Those who build
The grandest
    Cathedrals
Have the
    Gravest doubts.

Self-Righteous Wound

Whenever there
    Is a choice
People are
    More important
Than principles.

Were You There?

Compassion
    Is a
Tender pain,
    More important
Than righteous
    Disdain.

Who?

Who made you
    Made you well.
It's important
    That you don't
Go to pieces.

Human

A little virtue
    Will never
Hurt you.

And a bit of vice
    Is sometimes
Nice.

Tomorrow

Do-dreams
    Are the
Procrastinations
    Of life
Realized
    In time.

Quotations

Why quote?
    Let me
Be credible
    In my own
Right;
    Sure enough
To speak thoughts
    Without crutches.

Infinitude

Knowledge
    Is
Finite;
    Ignorance
Is
    Infinite.

Choice

"Oh God!
    I didn't know
What I
    Was doing"
Is often
    A choice
That makes
    Anything
Possible.

Atomic Detente

A-ha!
    I can kill you
More
    Than you
Can
    Kill me!

Human Logic

Opinions
    Are personal
Prejudices
    Backed by
Facts based
    On the
Experience
    Of one.

Facts
    Are mathematical
Observations
    Extracted from
Experience
    And based
Upon what
    Has been done.

Conclusions
    Arrive at
The marriage
    Of facts
And opinions
    Blessed by
The votes
    Of some.

Results
    Are ignored
Until forced
    Upon us
As the
    Inevitable
Offspring—
Awesome.

Part Four

The Poet as Minister and Theologian

Be or Be Not

If God be,
    Then He made me;
And why?
    And why did He
Make me so?

If God be,
    Then He made me
A maker;
    And why, why,
Do I make things so?

If God be not;
    No need to seek
Or use to cry;
    If God be not,
There's only "I."

If God be not
    Then each is only "I,"
And why, oh why
    Should I hear your cry?
If God be not.

But, God is;
    His word made me,
And that is why
    I seek and ask,
And why I hear your cry.

God Was There

The fingers,
    The folded hands
Weathered by
    A hundred seasons
Of storm and sun,
    Leathered and gnarled
Eternal as the
    Deep-grained strength
Of split-rail fences;
    The knuckles,
Huge and splayed
    By years of straining toil;
A webbing of tendons
    Mapping the strength
Of steel
    In those great hands.
I could feel
    In his furrowed face
The strength of
    Pasture granite boulders,
And the patience
    Of the hills was
In the arched
    Power of his
Bowed back and
    Sloping shoulders;
His noble head,
    Bent, and silvered
In the morning sun
    Slanting through
The windows
    Into the pew
Of his small
    Country church.
The smell of
    Old varnished wainscot
And altar flowers
    From the fields
Mixed faintly

      With wood smoke
And farm folk
      Who gathered
To worship;

A green bottle-fly
      Buzzed and bumped
The sunlit
      Window-silence
During the pastor's
      Quiet prayer;
Bent heads,
      Folded hands,
Sunlit silence,
      Buzzing fly,
And God
      Was there.

Out of Eden

You are
    In intruder;
Walk softly
    With care,
For you alone
    Are the
Piece that
    Does not fit;
You are
    The only one
Whose purpose
    And place
Cannot be
    Determined
In the matrix
    Of stars
And worlds
    And minutiae;
You alone
    Have been left
To your own
    Devices,
And you alone
    Can determine—
Make plans
    Of your own;
Here,
    You are
An intruder;
    Walk softly
And search
    With care,
That you
    May find,
And finding,
    Learn how
And what
    To be.

Salt

Ah, Lot,
    Was it
God?
    Or chance?

The circumstance
    By which
We leave
    The known,
The good,
    The bad,
And go
    We know not
Where—
    Would lead
Us each
    To ask
By whom
    Or what
Our Lot
    Is really
Cast.

Aureole

Some say,
    God gave
Only
    Half a
Love
    When love
Was made,
    And hungry
Journeyed we
    Through
Life
    To find
The price
    He paid;
That half
    A love
In hunger,
    Bestowed
Upon another,
    Brings
Love whole
    Upon
The loved
    And upon
The lover;
    That,
Love's labours,
    Freely lost,
Will fill
    The losers
Soul,
    And soft
Will be
    The radiance
Of love's
    Bright
Aureole.

To the Prisoner

Quiet,
    My soul;
Be at rest,
    Blessed rest
Within—
    For,
You are
    The accuser
And
    The accused;
The driver
    And
The driven;
    The inexcused,
The unforgiven;
    Forgiveness
Unaccepted;

The power
    Of
Phantom
    Hands
Holds your
    Soul—
Keeps your
    Knots,
Denies your
    Freedom,
Your
    Wholeness.

God smiled
    Eons ago—
Understanding
    What makes
Us so—
    That we
Will not
    Accept

The peace
    We proclaim.

Everything's
    All right.
Quiet,
    My soul;
Be at rest—
    Blessed rest
Within;
    It is for
Freedom
    That we
Are free.

We Both Know

It's a long
    Journey
In a moment
    From here
To there,
    And your
Dimming eyes
    Are asking
Me—
    Where?
    Where?
And all
    I can do
Is offer
    A prayer—
And the
    Parting squeeze
Of our hands.

Charon

>y you
>   Up there!
> r, where-
>   Ever.
> . bright
>   And tender
> Soul
>   Just arrived—
> I buried
>   My friend
> Today.

Catharsis

The Mass
    For the
Dead
    Seems often
A delayed
    Expiation
For the
    Living.

Mystery

I did not
    Dream,
Or deem
    It of
Consequence,
    That life
Should go,
    Or arrive
Some place
    Hence
In time;
    That it
Should be
    At all—
Is mystery
    Enough
In universe
    For my
Theology.

When You Go

What you
    Think
You have—
    You can
Neither own
    Nor keep.
What you
    Leave,
You know not—
    For
You leave
    Only
Relationships
    Remembered.

Reformation

God made
    All things
So that
    They would not
Last forever,
    But needs
Must
    Wear away
And die—
    And be
Renewed,
    Replaced,
Reformed,
    And born
Again.

All's Well

Muffled-
    Measured chiming
Of great bronze
    Bells in the village
Church tower;
    Chiming time
For the day
    And catching up
The lost hour;
    Sounding faint
Beyond my door
    Through dismal fog
And unrelenting
    Downpour
In the
    Brooding dimness
Of the day:
    An "All's well,"
Assurance

    Through the
Rushing silence;
    Warm sound
Of community
    In the midst
Of isolation.

Nativity

Light
    That curves
And hollows
    Limb-lines
Curled and
    Shadowed
To texture
    Bright warmth—
Brushing,
    Scarcely touching,
Edging with halo
    The figure,
Unseen-seen,
    That bends
And kneels
    In hovering pain
Pitifully
    Sheltering her fruit
From the
    Pouring light
Of star rain.

Ever-Beyond

God defined
    Becomes finite,
Framed, enshrined,
    And captive of
My finite mind;
    But the Almighty
Moves infinite
    And unframed;
The maker of
    Everything
I've named.

What I've defined
    Is definite
And knowable,
    Framed and confined;
While here
    In the
Ever-beyond
    God moves undefined
Forever infinite;
    Within my seeking
And beyond my sight.

Madonna

Sunday,
    During the service,
I watched them
    Watching
As she walked by.
    She carried
Her child asleep,
    Sweet
Innocent head
    Cuddled
In the curve
    Of her shoulder.

"How could she?"
    "I wonder?"
A tear,
    "How sweet,"
"Adopted?"
    "So right!"
A smile;
    What a beautiful
Sight—
    For the head
Was ebony
    And the shoulder
White.

Ecumene

There's
    Only us;
We're all
    In the
Same boat;
    "The," book
Is a book of
    Relations,
Theirs,
    Yours and mine;
What else matters?
    Perfection,
Or lack of it,
    Lies among us,
Within us;
    Those wishing
Perfect relations
    Must pay
The price;
    Everyone else
Expects
    And desires
The imperfect.

Biz

I thought
    A theology,
As someone
    Did
Originally,
    My word
Against his;
    And in the
Silence—
    A celestial
Chuckle
    Over this
Whole
    Theology
Biz.

Naming His Call

Man is not here
    Because of God;
God is here
    Because of man.

Man's grief and joy
    Is himself, and
Wherever he walks
    He foot-prints, "Why?"

"Why, and why, and why?"
    And wondering why,
He bells this ancient wonder,
    His haunting wonder cry.

The awesome surmise
    In his gift alone;
To wonder and ask why,
    Naming the clues his wonder finds.

Man is not here
>   Because of God;
God is here
>   Because of man.

Still Waters

Beat me,—
>   Pummel my soul,
Pain me awake,
>   Haunt me asleep.

Call me,
>   Accuse me,
>   Drive me,
Grant me a cause
>   And causes to
Confusion.

Tell me again
>   And yet again,
The dragging sorrows
>   Of the world,
And break over
>   My defenseless head
The flail that beats
>   Both ways at once.

Dear God,—I cry;
>   Just once,
Just once to lie
>   The green pastures,
And deep, deep,
>   To drink their peace
And walk beside
>   The still, still waters.

Ecumenicity

Salad bowl meeting:
    Tossed salad;
        Cut glass bowl—
And the carefully minced
    Speech of collared clergymen
Deftly hiding in the niceties
    Of correct speech,
        Correct clothing,
            And correct conduct.
Nothing could be
    Quite as good
        As tossed salad
            At a salad-bowl meeting.

Holy Grail

The miracle of the
Loaves and fishes
        was
Not so much
Bread and meat
    As
Love and wishes.

Not so much
Of mystery,
    As
Hunger shared
    In
Chaliced hearts
    And
Common dishes.

These Faces I See

These faces I see
    At the table divine,
Breaking their bread
    Where I now break mine.

They share the hope
    Of light and life,
Seeking Thy peace
    In their constant strife.

And who am I,
    O' God above,
To feel their hope
    And share their love?

I cannot seek;
    Thy face I shall not see,
'Til in these faces roundabout
    I find communion here with Thee.

The Last Laugh

        Death,
Smile as I pray,
    Robed, I stand
And give this nod
    To your moribund clay.
Could you not wink one eye
    At the stifled sob and cry?

The seed is sown!
    You are your own—
Terrestrial—terrestrial,
    Mortal mortality
And Death
    With no sense of humor.

These souls have already parted;
    Yours and hers,
Theirs and yours,
    Mine and thine,
Mahogany and satin,
    Purple and pine,
Perchance bronze bedded.

And music—
    Quiet and old;
As shoes that are worn.
    You, quiet and cold,
Last and first morn.

So, robed, I stand
    To pray and give this nod
To your house-for-rent of clay.
    Can you not smile as I pray,
Or wink an eye
    At the hue and cry?
And "Hello!" to God,
    As we pray good-bye.

Home Body

If I lay me
    Down to sleep,
Dare ask Him
    My soul
To keep
    While I
Am not at home?
    If I die
So far away,
    And He
My soul
    Should take;—
When I return
    How shall
I wake?
    Where shall
I go
    In the,
"To-and-fro,"
    That I—
Myself
    May not
Forsake?

"The Lord Is My Shepherd"

And this is Man;
    Turned and tickled,
Ravished and running.
    Hidden unheard.

Pavlovian funning;
    Sell! Sell! Sell!
By any means;
    Flash the neon cunning.

Run, Sheep, Run!
    Running, running, running;
Mass communication
    Mass strangers,
        Mass music thrumming.

Cathedral souls;
    Concerned hearts,
And anxious people—
    Running, running, running.

For the people are sheep,
    And the people are cunning,
But the Lord's my Shepherd,
    And God's not running.

Committal Day

Low gray
    And rain, driven;
Slanted before the wind
    In sheets,
Beating in upon
    Everything.
The sodden earth pelted
    Forwards and backwards
By sudden gusts
    And twists.
Dark, dark the heavens,
    Cheerless and raw
The November chill.
    This rain gutters
And suddenly runs
    With a thousand feet
Across the roof;
    It rivulets along the
Curbs and streets
    With liquid turning sounds,
And beats a
    Melancholy music—
A mourning song
    For the season past.

Each Other

Turn, and turn, and turn,
    And yet again—These seasons
Suns, stars and
    Full orbed moons
That come and go—
    These days and years
Patterned into life.

Sequence and con-sequence;
    A "Present"
With a "Past" and "Future;"
    And "If," and "Is," and "Therefore;"
And we understand;
    Struck light of mind!
        We see
We see the Reason
    And Reason comes into
        Being.

Humans being!
    Reasonable human beings;
Different and yet the same;
    All other forms different—
Because Reason came into Being—
    Patterned into life
        By sequence—
Sequence, and con-sequence
    And Law.

By Law we understand!
    We understand
The turning of the seasons,
    The suns, stars,
And full orbed moons,
    Sequence and con-sequence;
And we can reason;
    So much so, that
Only reasonable beings are sane.

What a glory in being!
    In being because of Law
And by Law.
    In being to reason,
In reason to walk
    The inner depths
Of meaning and purpose
    To discover
How the thing works;
    And by what Law it operates.

Span the ages of man,
    Count the Laws of reason
And being.
    Laws of gravity and aerodynamics;
Laws of engineering and physics;
    Laws of nature used by man;
Laws of heat and cold;
    Laws of energy and power;
Laws of molecules and atoms;
    Laws of protons and electrons;
Laws of inner space,
    And laws of outer space.
By Law we understand,
    And reason, we have our being.

So we fly without wings;
    We walk in space;
We plumb the depths
    Of ancient seas,
And tunnel the rich
    Crust of the earth.
We mine with music
    The unseen waves,
And cast our electronic
    Image in countless lands;
Because we are reasonable beings,
    And we understand the Law.

But—there is a Law
    Of each other;
A Law of Prophets and Priests;
    A Law of Humans being—
Laws of Spirit,
    And Humans relating;
As well as things,
    And things relating.
There is an hypothesis
    Of the soul
Just as sound as
    That of the sciences—
The "If," the "Is," and "Therefore"
    That come when
Reason and Being come
    To the Human.

By Law, given and recorded,
    Forgotten and found—
Is all of Human Being
    Patterned into life
By sequence,
    Sequence and con-sequence,
        And Law?
Law which brings to life
    The "Ought"
Against the "Is" and
    The Spirit by which we live?

Laws are commandments,
    And such as these are life
And the meaning of life.
    The Law of the God of Moses
Is just as sure as
    The Law of gravity;
And the Law of Religious Faith
    As sure as the Law
Of inner and outer space.

    And so we fly without wings,
        And walk in space,
Mine with music
        The unseen waves,
And tunnel the ancient seas;
        But ah!—each other.